BACKYARD WILDLIFE

Turtles

by Emily Green

BELLWETHER MEDIA • MINNEAPOLIS, MN

Note to Librarians, Teachers, and Parents:

Blastoff! Readers are carefully developed by literacy experts and combine standards-based content with developmentally appropriate text.

Level 1 provides the most support through repetition of high-frequency words, light text, predictable sentence patterns, and strong visual support.

Level 2 offers early readers a bit more challenge through varied simple sentences, increased text load, and less repetition of high-frequency words.

Level 3 advances early-fluent readers toward fluency through increased text and concept load, less reliance on visuals, longer sentences, and more literary language.

Level 4 builds reading stamina by providing more text per page, increased use of punctuation, greater variation in sentence patterns, and increasingly challenging vocabulary.

Level 5 encourages children to move from "learning to read" to "reading to learn" by providing even more text, varied writing styles, and less familiar topics.

Whichever book is right for your reader, Blastoff! Readers are the perfect books to build confidence and encourage a love of reading that will last a lifetime!

This edition first published in 2011 by Bellwether Media, Inc.

No part of this publication may be reproduced in whole or in part without written permission of the publisher. For information regarding permission, write to Bellwether Media, Inc., Attention: Permissions Department, 5357 Penn Avenue South, Minneapolis, MN 55419.

Library of Congress Cataloging-in-Publication Data
Green, Emily K., 1966–
Turtles / by Emily Green.
    p. cm. — (Blastoff! readers. Backyard wildlife)
Summary: "Developed by literacy experts for students in kindergarten through grade three, this book introduces turtles to young readers through leveled text and related photos"—Provided by publisher.
Includes bibliographical references and index.
ISBN 978-1-60014-448-6 (hardcover : alk. paper)
1. Turtles—Juvenile literature. I. Title.
QL666.C5G74 2010
597.92—dc22

2010010686

Text copyright © 2011 by Bellwether Media, Inc. BLASTOFF! READERS and associated logos are trademarks and/or registered trademarks of Bellwether Media, Inc.

Printed in the United States of America, North Mankato, MN.

080110   1162

Contents

Turtles are animals with shells. Shells cover their backs and bellies.

Turtles have **scales** on their shells. The scales are bumpy or smooth.

bumpy scales

smooth scales

Many turtles have spots or **patterns** on their scales.

Turtles live on land or in water. They move slowly on land.

Some turtles are good swimmers. They rest in the sun to warm their bodies.

Most turtles eat plants and **insects**. A turtle grabs food with its **beak**.

beak

Turtles do not have teeth. They use their **jaws** to bite and chew.

Turtles do not take care of their young. Baby turtles must find food and stay safe.

19

Turtles hide in their shells when they **sense** danger. They come out again when it is safe. Welcome back, turtle!

Glossary

beak—the name for the mouths of some animals such as birds and turtles

insects—small animals with six legs and hard outer bodies; insect bodies are divided into three parts.

jaws—the bones that form the mouth of an animal

patterns—shapes and designs that repeat; some animals have patterns on their bodies.

scales—hard plates that cover the bodies of some animals

sense—to become aware of

To Learn More

AT THE LIBRARY

Berger, Melvin. *Look Out for Turtles!* New York, N.Y.: HarperCollins, 1992.

Falwell, Cathryn. *Turtle Splash! Countdown at the Pond.* New York, N.Y.: Greenwillow Books, 2001.

Fredericks, Anthony D. *Near One Cattail: Turtles, Logs, and Leaping Frogs.* Nevada City, Calif.: Dawn Publications, 2005.

ON THE WEB

Learning more about turtles is as easy as 1, 2, 3.

1. Go to www.factsurfer.com.

2. Enter "turtles" into the search box.

3. Click the "Surf" button and you will see a list of related Web sites.

With factsurfer.com, finding more information is just a click away.

Index

The images in this book are reproduced through the courtesy of: Eric Isselee, front cover; Minden Pictures/ Masterfile, p. 5; Ryan M. Bolton, p. 7; Juan Martinez, pp. 7 (left), 9, 13; Jody Dingle, p. 7 (right); Juniors Bildarchiv/Alamy, p. 11; Juniors Bildarchiv/Photolibrary, pp. 15, 17; Michael Francis/Animals Animals – Earth Scenes, p. 19; Bull's-Eye Arts, p. 21.